Berry
the
Blue Whale

by Jenny Schreiber

Berry the Blue Whale
Discover the Magnificent Underwater World of Blue Whales
(Pre-Reader)

In Association with:
Elite Online Publishing
63 East 11400 South
Suite #230
Sandy, UT 84070
EliteOnlinePublishing.com

ISBN: 978-1-961801-00-4

Berry
the
Blue Whale

by Jenny Schreiber

Meet Berry the Blue Whale.

He is the largest

animal on earth!

Berry can grow to be as long
as three school buses.

Berry weighs as much as
25 elephants.

25 X

Berry was born underwater
and was close to the size of
a big truck.

Berry grew very quickly by
drinking his mother's milk,
which is high in fat.
Berry is a mammal.

Berry has a unique spout or
blowhole on top of his head.
He uses this hole to
breathe oxygen.

Berry is an amazing
swimmer. He can swim up to
20 miles per hour
(32 kilometers per hour).

Berry is an amazing diver.
He can dive as deep as
1,000 feet
(305 meters)
to find food.

When Berry dives, he can
hold his breath for around
10 to 20 minutes.
Sometimes
up to 30 minutes.

Berry has a special way of eating.
He opens his huge mouth and gulps
in tons of tiny shrimp-like animals
called krill.

Berry filters out the shrimp using
baleen plates in his mouth.
Like a strainer catches pasta
in the kitchen.

Berry is very loud.
He makes deep, low-frequency
sounds that can travel for
miles underwater.

Berry uses the sounds to help him communicate with other whales.

Berry has a huge heart,

as big as a small car!

Berry is a gentle giant.
Even though he is huge, he only
eats tiny creatures and doesn't
harm people.

Berry and other blue whales can
be found in oceans all around
the world.

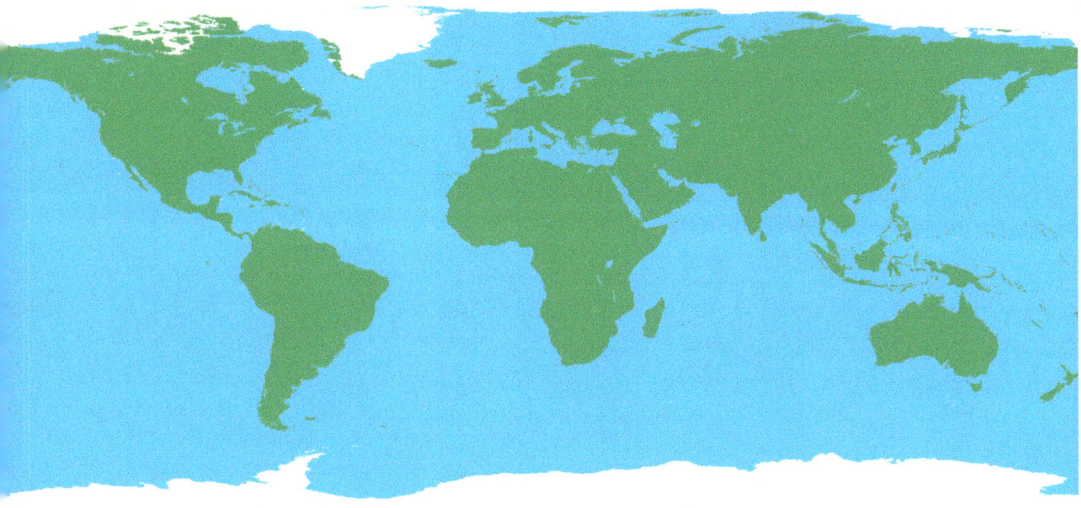

Berry migrates long distances
each year, traveling from cold
waters near the north and south
poles to warmer waters
near the equator.

Blue whales are a protected species, which means they need our help to stay safe.

People around the world are working together to protect Berry and his amazing family and their ocean habitats.

The End

Read More Animal books
by Jenny Schreiber

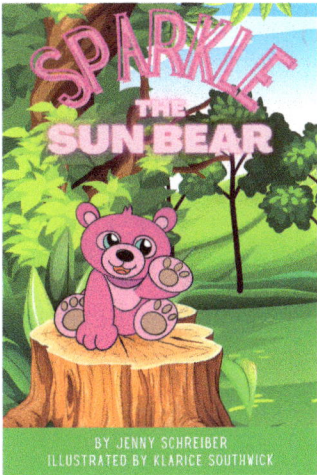

Sparkle the Sun Bear

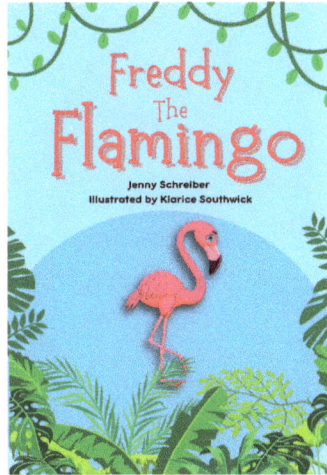

Freddy the Flamingo

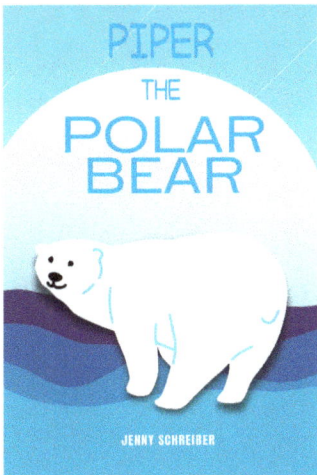

Piper the Polar Bear

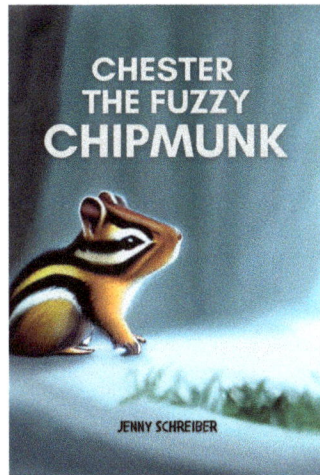

Chester the
Fuzzy Chipmunk

Animal Facts Children's Book Series

Paige the Panda Bear

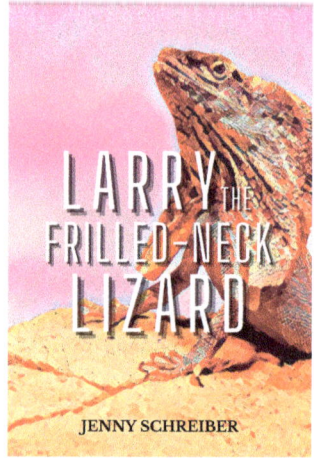

Larry the
Frilled-Neck Lizard

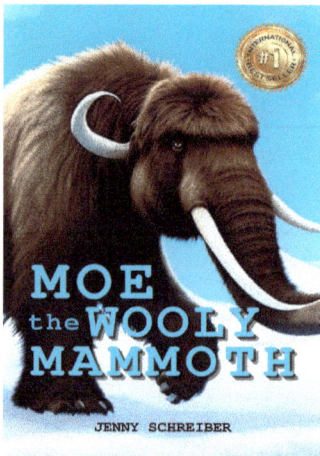

Moe the
Wooly Mammoth

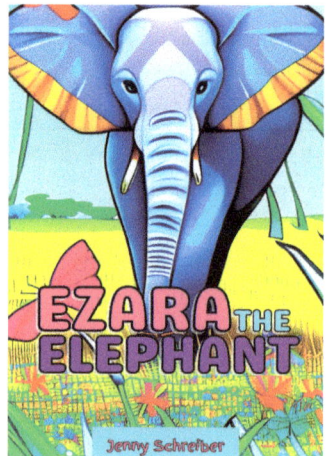

Ezara the Elephant

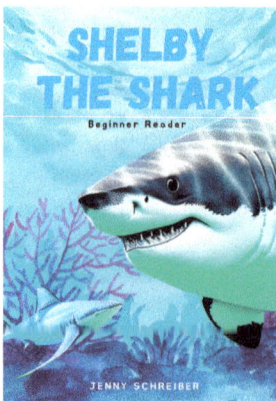

Shelby the Shark